NOW YOU CAN READ ABOUT...

CREATURES of the NIGHT

TEXT BY RITA GRAINGE

ILLUSTRATED BY BOB BAMPTON

BRIMAX BOOKS • NEWMARKET • ENGLAND

When we are asleep at night, many creatures are awake. They hunt for food in the dark. These animals rest during the day.

Wood mice come out at night. They feed on seeds and berries. Look out, mouse! The owl is coming.

The loris eats birds. It catches them at night when the birds are asleep in their nests.

The mouse deer is found in Africa and Asia. It is a very shy animal. It feels safer at night when most of its enemies are sleeping.

Look at this strange creature. It is a giant anteater. If it lives near houses, it hunts at night. It is scared of people.

Most night creatures
hunt alone.

The linsang lives
a lonely life.
It hunts birds,
lizards and frogs
during the night.

The moonrat is
very shy. No one
knows much about
it. Moonrats keep
away from other
animals. They
feed on insects
and worms.

The leopard gecko is a reptile. Look at its large eyes. It feeds on insects at night.

These hunting dogs live in the wild in Africa. They hunt in groups called packs. On moonlit nights they hunt antelope and zebra.

Hunting in the dark is not easy. Many creatures of the night have senses which help them.

The tarsier has very large eyes. These help it to see better than most animals. When a tarsier rests, it keeps one eye open.

Ground beetles eat insects and snails. They have very good eyesight. This helps them find their prey.

This raccoon is
fishing. It uses
its paws to feel
the water move.
This means a fish
is coming.

Moles spend most
of the time under
ground. They have
tiny eyes. Their
whiskers feel
movements in
the soil.

Some creatures have a strong
sense of smell.

When night moths
smell the scent
of a bat, they
fly away.

A polecat uses
its sense of
smell to hunt
mice and rabbits.

Look at this
armadillo. When
it smells anything
in the ground, it
digs very fast.
It holds its breath
while digging.

Some snakes have a special sense to help them hunt in the dark. These snakes are called pit vipers. They have a pit on either side of the head near the eye. The snake senses changes in heat. It also knows where the heat is coming from. Then it glides towards its prey and injects it with poison.

Other night creatures use their ears to help them find food and to keep out of danger.

The aye-aye taps on a branch and listens. It finds a hollow under the bark. Then it nibbles at the wood and scoops out insects. Look at its long middle finger.

A fox can move its ears forwards and backwards.

Bats are nearly blind. When they fly, they sense changes in the air around them. Then they know when they are close to something. This special sense also helps bats to find food.

Can you see the barn owl? It is looking for food. Night birds have soft edges and tips to their wing feathers. They make no sound as they fly. When the owl swoops down, its prey does not hear it coming.

Bird-eating spiders make no sound when they move. They eat insects and small lizards. They do not eat birds.

This wild cat moves slowly over its home ground. The genet can remember all that it smells and feels. This helps it to move about safely at night.

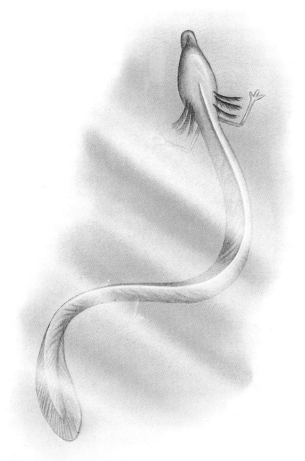

This is an olm. It is always dark in its cave home. Olms are blind. Their eyes are hidden beneath the skin.

At the bottom of the ocean there is no light. It is always night time for the creatures who live there. These fish have rows of lights along their belly. These help them to see one another in the dark. The long thin creature is a viper fish. The others are hatchet fish.

The penguins
live on the ice
in the Antarctic.
In winter it is
dark all day. It is
also very cold.

In winter in the Arctic the polar
bear is a creature of the dark.
The sun never shines. When it is
winter in the Arctic it is summer
in the Antarctic.

Creatures of the night do not have darkness to hide them when they sleep during the day. They use other ways of hiding.

A frogmouth bird hides by keeping very still. Look at the tree bark. Can you see the moth?

Wombats make burrows under ground. Some burrows are half a mile long.

Most creatures of
the night have
dark colours. This
helps them to hide.
It is not easy to
see a kiwi in the
evening light.

Some creatures
have strong
colours. A skunk's
white stripes warn
other animals to
keep away.

Fireflies flash
messages to each
other.

Many birds fly to other countries
during the night. They use the
moon and stars to guide them.
During the day they come down
to earth to rest and feed. Look at
these night flyers. The bird on
the post is a tern. A kingfisher
is diving into the water.

It is easy to watch animals during the day. It is not so easy at night. The darkness makes it hard for us to learn about creatures of the night. A special light is shone on these badgers so that people can film them.

Here are some creatures of the night. What is special about them?